NATIONAL GEOGRAPHIC
KIDS

weird
but
true! 4

NATIONAL
GEOGRAPHIC

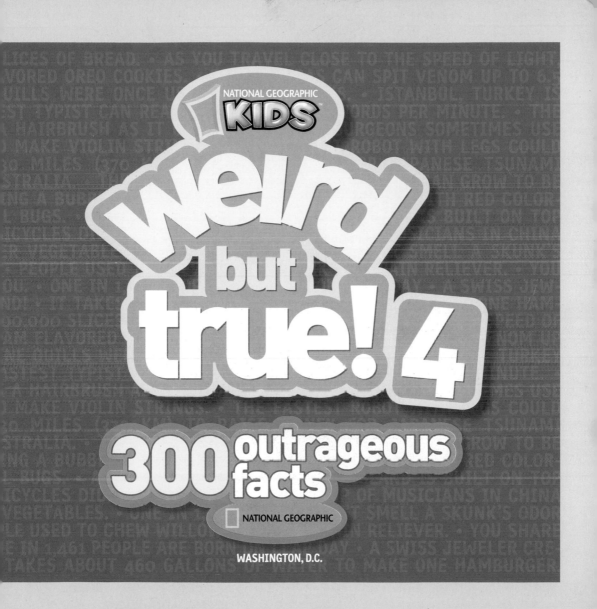

NATIONAL GEOGRAPHIC
KIDS

weird but true! 4

300 outrageous facts

NATIONAL GEOGRAPHIC

WASHINGTON, D.C.

Visit us online at nationalgeographic.com/books

For librarians and teachers: ngchildrensbooks.org

More for kids from National Geographic: kids.nationalgeographic.com

For information about special discounts for bulk purchases, please contact
National Geographic Books Special Sales: ngspecsales@ngs.org

For rights or permissions inquiries, please contact National Geographic Books
Subsidiary Rights: ngbookrights@ngs.org

Paperback ISBN: 978-1-4263-1020-1
Library ISBN: 978-1-4263-1021-8
Scholastic ISBN: 978-1-4263-1263-2

Printed in China
12/CCOS/1

Some jellyfish glow.

THERE'S A MUSHROOM NAMED AFTER SPONGEBOB SQUAREPANTS.

Deep-fried **Kool-Aid** is sold as a snack at a county fair in California, U.S.A.

LEMONS CAN POWER LIGHTBULBS.

A man skipped a rock on water **51** times in one throw.

The last thing **Elvis ate** was **ice cream and cookies.**

MILLIONS OF YEARS AGO, **THERE WAS A BIRD** IN AUSTRALIA THAT WEIGHED AS MUCH AS A **POLAR BEAR.**

More earthquakes occur in Alaska than in any other U.S. state.

Fire trucks were originally painted

The **death's-head moth** has a **skull-shaped design** on its body.

red because that was the cheapest color.

Teams of soccer-playing **robots** compete every year at the **RoboCup.**

MUSICIANS PERFORMED A HIGH-FREQUENCY **ROCK CONCERT** IN AUSTRALIA THAT **ONLY DOGS COULD HEAR.**

A HORSE NEVER BREATHES THROUGH ITS MOUTH, EXCEPT IN EMERGENCIES.

Ants
AS BIG AS **THIS TOY CAR** ONCE MARCHED ON EARTH.

Hummingbird **nests** are about the size of a **golf ball.**

Laid end-to-end, all of the **iPhones** and **iPads** sold in one year would stretch halfway around the **Earth.**

There's a condition that makes it impossible for some people to recognize faces.

The **average strawberry has 200 seeds.**

No red M&Ms were produced between 1976 and 1987.

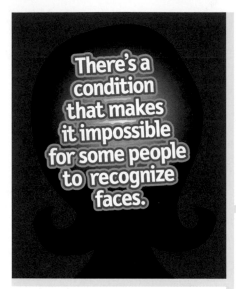

BOX JELLYFISH HAVE EYES BUT NO **BRAIN.**

ANTARCTICA HAS **24** HOURS OF DAYLIGHT FOR PART OF THE **SUMMER.**

SOME LOBSTERS ARE ELECTRIC BLUE.

Your hands have

26 percent of the bones in your body.

There are 27 bones in each hand,

including your wrist.

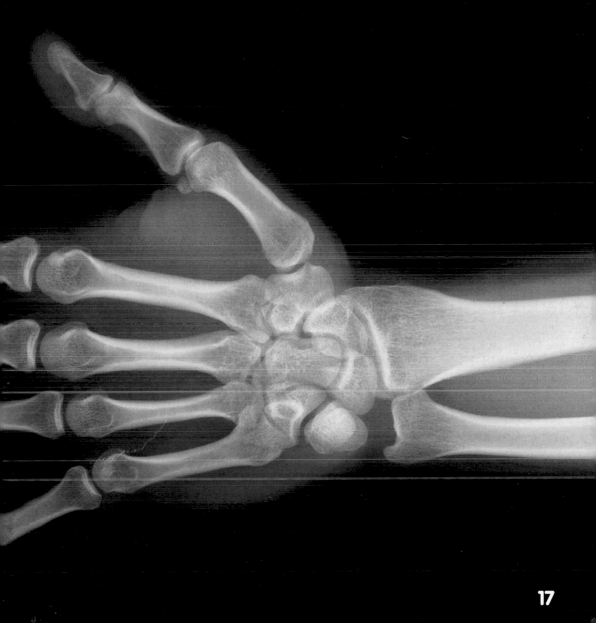

TERMITES EVOLVED FROM COCKROACHES.

GIRLS SEND AND RECEIVE MORE THAN TWICE AS MANY TEXT MESSAGES AS BOYS.

Competitors race tricked-out **portable potties** at the annual **outhouse races** in Nevada, U.S.A.

Russian supermarkets carry **caviar-flavored** potato chips.

Some Ice Age people used **human skulls** as drinking **cups.**

The **moon** can look red during a **lunar eclipse.**

The first **stop signs** were **black-and-white.**

The Frisbee was originally named the **Pluto Platter.**

IF A SPACE SHUTTLE
COULD TRAVEL TO
THE SUN
IT WOULD TAKE ABOUT
220 DAYS TO
GET THERE.

THERE'S AN ANNUAL

REDHEAD FESTIVAL
IN THE NETHERLANDS.

SOME **CHICKENS** ARE **BORN HALF-MALE, HALF-FEMALE.**

A
group
of
owls
is called a
parliament.

Some **cave-dwelling** **salamanders** don't have **eyes.**

PREHISTORIC HUMANS **CHEWED** TREE RESIN AS CHEWING GUM.

Some **bats'** hearing is strong enough to detect the sound of a beetle walking on a leaf.

THE LONGEST NONSTOP FLIGHT BY A BIRD IS EIGHT DAYS.

A pair of **ruby slippers** from *The Wizard of Oz* sold for more than **$660,000.**

THE UNIVERSE IS FLAT.

More than **5 billion** green **Monopoly houses** have been manufactured since the **game** was introduced in 1935.

A white stork in Germany mysteriously turned blue.

There are about ***three pounds*** *of bacteria* (1.4 kg) *living in your stomach.*

BEES CAN SEE ULTRAVIOLET, YELLOW, BLUE, AND BLUE-GREEN, BUT NOT RED.

27

Each year about

1,000,000,000,000

000,000,000,000
snow crystals
drop from the sky.

Some **gorillas play tag.**

TAG, YOU'RE IT!

It's possible for a **seed** to blow across **the ocean** and **sprout** on another continent.

New Caledonian **crows** make right-handed and left-handed **tools.**

A NEW YORK ARTIST SELLS CLEAR CUBES **filled with trash** FOR AS MUCH AS $100.

Coughing while you get a shot can make it hurt less.

MOST BATS CAN'T TAKE FLIGHT FROM THE GROUND.

A dog named **Yoda** won the world's Ugliest Dog Contest.

A BEAVER COULD SWIM 16 LAPS IN AN OLYMPIC-SIZE POOL WITHOUT TAKING A BREATH.

CRABS ARE DISTANT RELATIVES OF SPIDERS.

LAS VEGAS, *Nevada, U.S.A.,* **IS THE BRIGHTEST SPOT** ON EARTH.

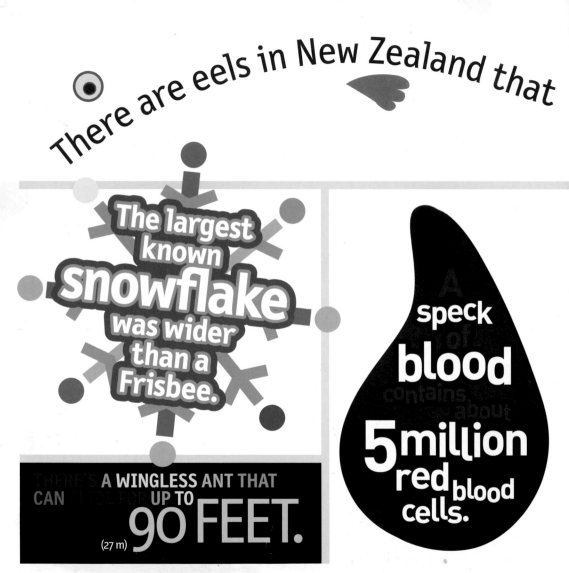

There are eels in New Zealand that

The largest known **snowflake** was wider than a Frisbee.

THERE'S **A WINGLESS** ANT THAT CAN GLIDE FOR UP **TO** **90** FEET.
(27 m)

A speck of **blood** contains about **5 million** **red** blood cells.

can live for more than 100 years.

A FAMILY OF FIVE RODE A **FIVE-SEAT BIKE** 6,439 **MILES** (10,363 km) **FROM KENTUCKY TO ALASKA, U.S.A.,** **IN ONE YEAR.**

COMPETITORS HURL THEIR OLD **CELL PHONES** FOR SPORT AT FINLAND'S ANNUAL **MOBILE PHONE THROWING CHAMPIONSHIPS.**

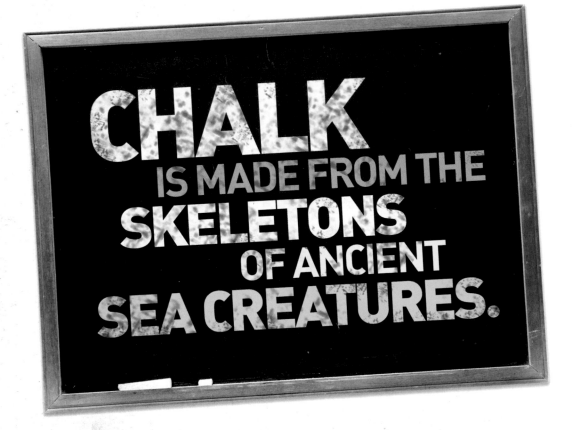

CHALK IS MADE FROM THE SKELETONS OF ANCIENT SEA CREATURES.

A
National
Geographic
Channel
team used
300
helium
balloons
to lift a
lightweight house—
with people inside!—
more than
two miles
into the air. (3.5 km)

INSPIRED BY
THE MOVIE *UP*

AN OCTOPUS HAS RECTANGULAR PUPILS.

When there's
thunder during
a snowstorm,
it's called

THUNDER-SNOW.

Odontophobia
is the fear of teeth.

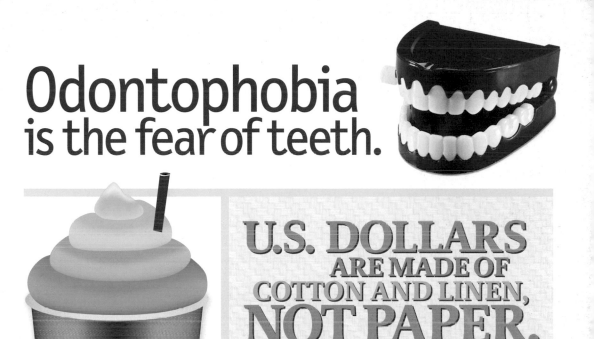

U.S. DOLLARS ARE MADE OF COTTON AND LINEN, NOT PAPER.

You can beat. **brain freeze** by pressing your tongue to the roof of your **mouth.**

Catfish have **ten times** more taste buds than people do.

PENGUIN DROPPINGS CAN BE pink.

YOU **GROW** FASTER IN THE **SUMMER** THAN YOU DO IN THE **FALL**.

There's a fruit named "stinking toe."

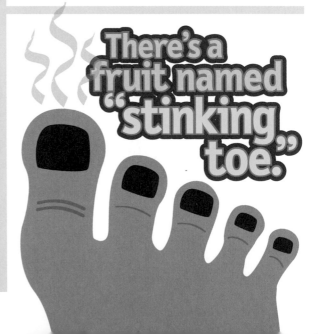

Elephants can swim for up to **6** hours without resting.

Some **sunspots**—magnetic fields on the sun—are bigger than **Earth.**

OUNCE FOR OUNCE, SOME **CATERPILLAR MEAT** CONTAINS **MORE PROTEIN** THAN **LEAN BEEF.**

A **150-METER**
(164-yard)
pool
atop a
55-story
hotel
IN SINGAPORE
is the
world's
LARGEST OUTDOOR
swimming pool
AT THAT HEIGHT.

Cockleshells are heart-shaped.

A **narwhal** uses its **tusk** to detect changes in the **weather**.

Ripe bananas glow blue under a black light.

A **MONTH** ON VENUS IS LONGER THAN A **DECADE** ON VENUS.

EVERY **BASEBALL** USED IN A **MAJOR-LEAGUE GAME** GETS RUBBED DOWN WITH **MUD** BEFORE THE GAME.

Bats' knees face backward.

IT TAKES
THOUSANDS OF YEARS
FOR LIGHT
TO TRAVEL FROM THE
SUN'S CORE
TO ITS SURFACE.

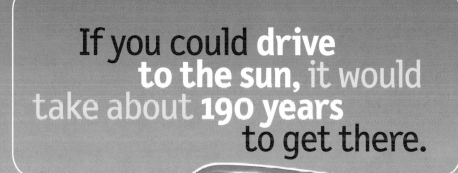

If you could **drive to the sun**, it would take about **190 years** to get there.

The **moon** weighs
81,000,000,000,000,000,000 tons.
(73,000,000,000,000,000,000 metric tons)

WATERMELONS ARE 92% WATER.

54

-40°F **-40°C**

-40° is the only temperature that is the same in Celsius and Fahrenheit.

A WOODPECKER
CAN PECK A TREE
UP TO 30 TIMES A SECOND.

Ostrich plumes were once worth *twice their weight in gold* in London, England.

A bridge built in Lima, Peru, is reportedly held together by egg whites.

More than **950 beetles** can live in a **sloth's fur** at one time.

You are **rarely** more than **six feet** (1.8 m) away from a spider.

THE WORLD'S **MOST** STOLEN FOOD IS CHEESE.

YOUR SKIN SHEDS AND REGROWS ONCE A MONTH.

A spatula that was lost on an astronaut's space walk is still floating **in space.**

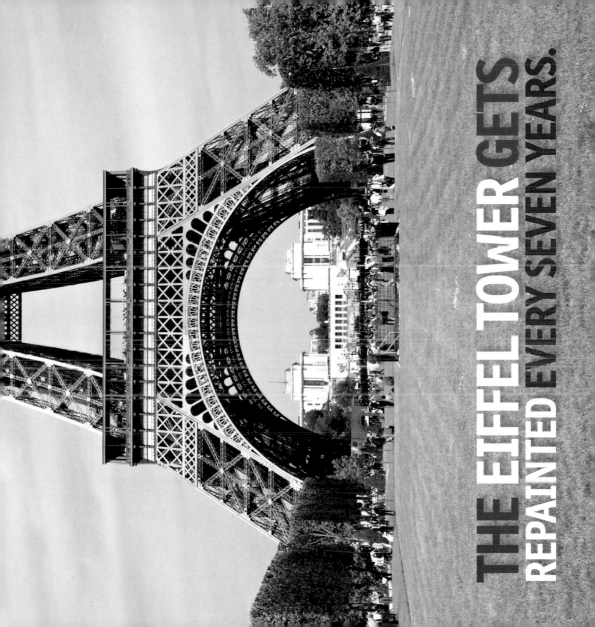

THE EIFFEL TOWER GETS
REPAINTED EVERY SEVEN YEARS.

A man wrote an entire **novel** without using the letter "e."

PROFESSIONAL WAKER-UPPERS ONCE GOT PAID TO BE HUMAN ALARM CLOCKS BY KNOCKING ON WINDOWS WITH POLES.

There is almost always an **even number of rows** on an ear of corn.

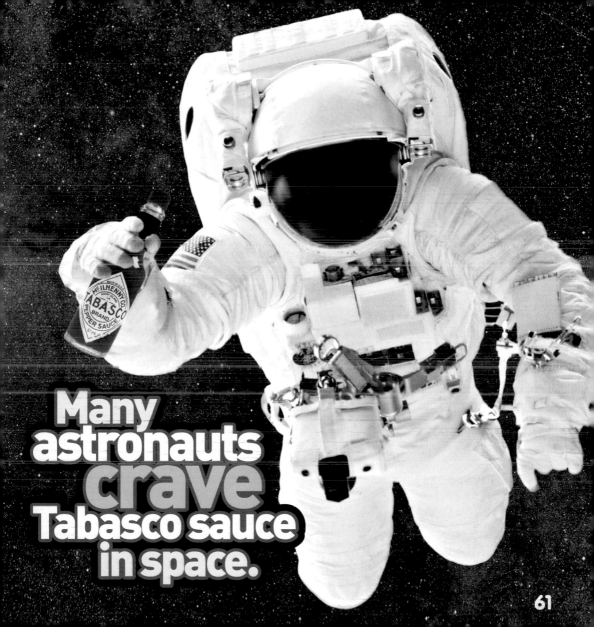

Many astronauts **crave** Tabasco sauce in space.

PIRANHAS BARK.

Sound travels **15 times faster** through **steel** than through **air.**

2012

SOME SPIDERS SPIN WEBS

Some musicians with amnesia can still remember how to play music.

2020

LONGER THAN TWO CITY BUSES!

A GROUP OF TURKEYS

TOADS DO NOT HAVE TEETH.

THE SPATULA-TAILED HUMMINGBIRD'S TAIL IS SO HEAVY THAT IT CAN ONLY FLY FOR A FEW SECONDS.

ONE OF JUPITER'S MOONS, CALLED EUROPA, MAY HAVE TWICE AS MUCH WATER AS ALL THE OCEANS ON EARTH.

SOME MAMMAL SPECIES GROW BIGGER IN COLD CLIMATES.

The first person arrested for speeding in the United States was driving **12 miles an hour** in 1899. (19 kph)

A kangaroo **rat** does not need to **drink water.**

At a restaurant in **Denmark,** you can order **an appetizer** made with **needles** from a **Douglas fir.**

THERE'S ENOUGH PAINT ON THE WORLD'S LARGEST PASSENGER JET TO COVER TEN BASKETBALL COURTS.

There is a **trap** designed to catch **Bigfoot** in a **forest** in Oregon, U.S.A.

THE WORLD'S FASTEST TYPIST CAN REACH SPEEDS OF 200 WORDS PER MINUTE.

Porcupine **quills** were once used as toothpicks.

A puppy in California, U.S.A., was so tiny it was smaller than an iPhone!

AT TWO WEEKS OLD

THE ENERGY IN **ONE BOLT OF LIGHTNING** COULD TOAST ABOUT **100,000 SLICES OF BREAD.**

AFGHANISTAN AND **AZERBAIJAN** ARE THE ONLY COUNTRIES THAT BEGIN, BUT DON'T END, WITH THE **LETTER A.**

90 percent of an **iceberg** is **underwater.**

A TEENAGER CREATED A **STAPLE CHAIN** THAT'S AS LONG AS A CRUISE SHIP.

There are twice as many chickens on Earth as people.

Moviemakers invented a new language for the made-up **Na'vi people** in the movie *Avatar.*

Snail slime can be used to soften skin.

Some **wasps** use pebbles as hammers to build their nests.

STOMACH ACID CAN DISSOLVE METAL.

NASCAR DRIVERS CAN LOSE 5 TO 10 (2.3 to 4.5 kg) POUNDS IN SWEAT DURING ONE RACE.

There's a
beach in the
Bahamas where you
can swim
with wild pigs.

Eleven

miles an hour *(17.7 kph)* is the **fastest** a vehicle has ever driven on the **moon—** that's about as fast as you ride a bike!

CANADA'S POSTAL CODE FOR THE NORTH POLE IS HOH OHO.

Santa Claus
North Pole
Hoh OHo
Canada

SOME PREHISTORIC PEOPLE USED MAMMOTH BONES TO BUILD THEIR HOMES.

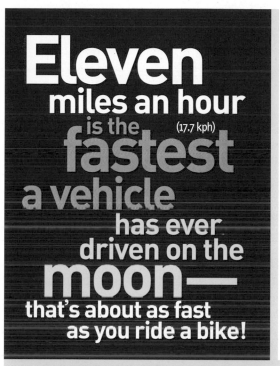

REPLICA OF HOME MADE FROM BONES

A
giant
anteater
is
6 feet
long, (1.8 m)
yet its
mouth
is as small
as a grape.

FUNGUS CAN GROW OUT OF A ZOMBIE ANT'S HEAD.

EWW, FUNGUS!

The world's most expensive gold coin sold for a whopping $7.4 million.

In Japan, the "OK" sign means "Pay me."

IT TAKES A
WET DOG LESS THAN A **SECOND** TO SHAKE OFF **HALF** OF THE **WATER** ON ITS FUR.

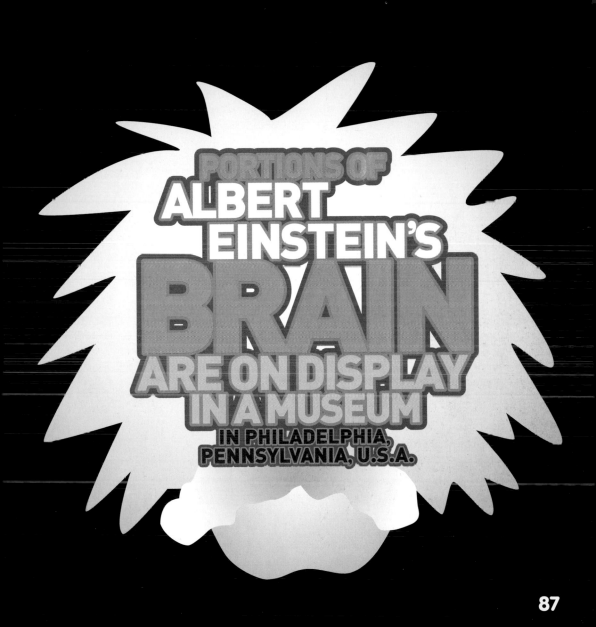

PORTIONS OF **ALBERT EINSTEIN'S** **BRAIN** ARE ON DISPLAY IN A MUSEUM IN PHILADELPHIA, PENNSYLVANIA, U.S.A.

Tasmanian devils sometimes **sneeze** to challenge other **devils to a fight.**

A FASHION **DESIGNER** CREATED A NEW **FABRIC** MADE ENTIRELY FROM **MILK.**

Silly Putty was used aboard **Apollo 8** to keep tools **from floating** around the ship.

TOOTHPASTE WAS ONCE MADE FROM CUTTLEFISH BONES.

THE FASTEST IS 5.66 SECONDS; A PERSON HAS EVER SOLVED A RUBIK'S CUBE A ROBOT DID IT FOUR-TENTHS OF A SECOND FASTER.

THE
100 YEARS' WAR

ACTUALLY LASTED 116 YEARS

(from 1337 to 1453).

A LUMP OF **GOLD** SMALL ENOUGH TO HOLD IN YOUR **HAND** CAN BE FLATTENED INTO A **SHEET** AS BIG AS A **TENNIS COURT.**

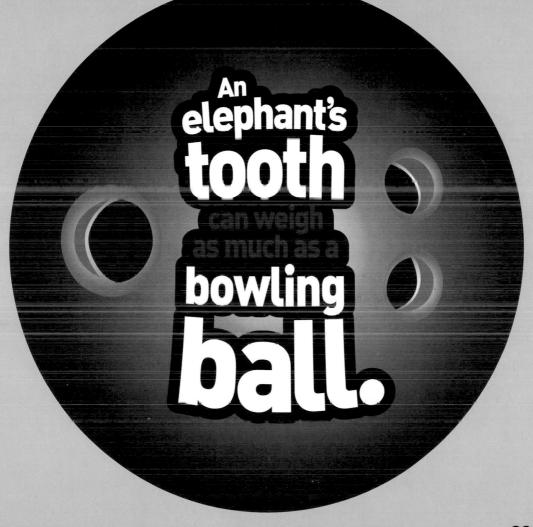

An elephant's tooth can weigh as much as a bowling ball.

During the rainy season, **the water spilling over Africa's Victoria Falls** could fill **1,635 Olympic-size swimming pools** in one hour.

The average **cherry tree** produces enough **fruit** every year to fill **28 pies.**

DUCT TAPE HAS BEEN USED TO REMOVE A WART.

DON'T TRY THIS AT HOME!

Butt🞅ns *were once made from* **mussel shells.**

THE BRAIN DOESN'T FEEL PAIN.

There is a toilet museum in South Korea shaped like a toilet bowl.

CROCODILES SWALLOW ROCKS TO HELP DIGEST THEIR FOOD.

PEOPLE IN **SCOTLAND** USED TO CURE **BUTTER** BY **BURYING** IT IN **PEAT BOGS** FOR **SEVEN YEARS.**

MILLIONS OF YEARS AGO, **AUSTRALIA'S DESERTS** WERE AS WET AND LUSH AS A **RAIN FOREST.**

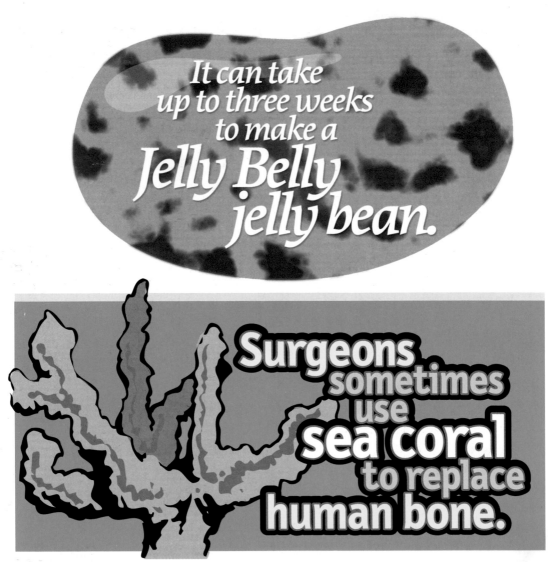

It can take
up to three weeks
to make a
Jelly Belly
jelly bean.

Surgeons
sometimes
use
sea coral
to replace
human bone.

A STUDY FOUND THAT **DAIRY COWS** MAY PRODUCE MORE **MILK** WHILE LISTENING TO **CLASSICAL MUSIC.**

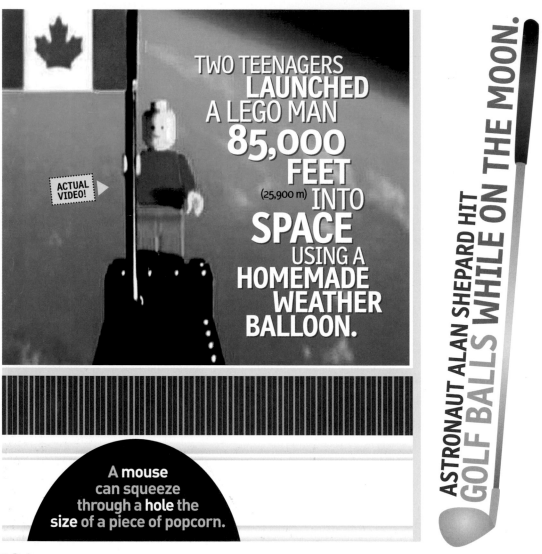

TWO TEENAGERS **LAUNCHED** A LEGO MAN **85,000 FEET** (25,900 m) INTO **SPACE** USING A **HOMEMADE WEATHER BALLOON.**

ACTUAL VIDEO!

A **mouse** can squeeze through a **hole** the **size** of a piece of popcorn.

ASTRONAUT ALAN SHEPARD HIT **GOLF BALLS WHILE ON THE MOON.**

DOLPHINS EVOLVED FROM EARLY ANCESTORS OF GIRAFFES AND CAMELS.

PEOPLE IN THE UNITED STATES EAT MORE BANANAS THAN APPLES AND ORANGES COMBINED.

AN ARTIST CREATED A ONE-TON, LIFE-SIZE MAMMOTH OUT OF RECYCLED FARM EQUIPMENT.

You can make paper out of dryer lint.

The Statue of Liberty's **torch** sways up to **5 inches** (12.7 cm) in the wind.

Artists in Italy created a ~~pink~~ stuffed **rabbit** big enough to see from space!

Wearing blue-tinted sunglasses may make you less hungry.

SCIENTISTS **FOUND A ONE-EYED "CYCLOPS" SHARK** IN MEXICO.

Most household **dust** contains dead skin.

MALE MICE **SING** TO **ATTRACT** POTENTIAL **MATES.**

After recycling almost all of their waste, one family of four was able to fit a year's worth of trash in a spaghetti sauce jar.

Pumice
is the
only rock
that can
float in water.

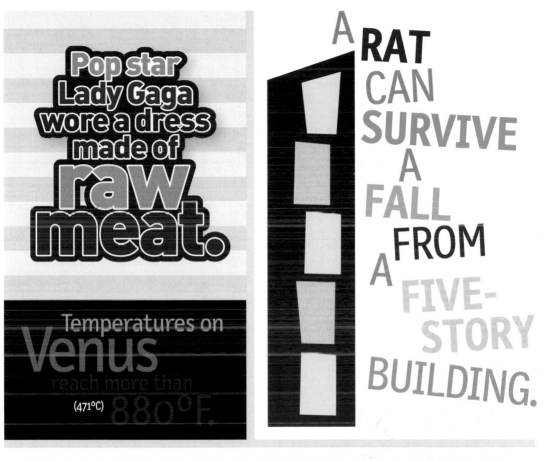

Pop star Lady Gaga wore a dress made of **raw meat.**

Temperatures on **Venus** reach more than (471°C) 880°F.

A **RAT** CAN **SURVIVE** A FALL FROM A **FIVE-STORY** BUILDING.

YOU MAY MAKE BETTER DECISIONS **WITH A FULL BLADDER.**

A
7-foot-9-inch
(2.1-m)
basketball
player
can
dunk
without
jumping.

THE RAINIEST PLACE
IN THE CONTINENTAL UNITED STATES
——ABERDEEN, WASHINGTON——
GETS **11 FEET**
(3.4 m)
OF RAIN
EVERY YEAR.
IF IT FELL ALL AT ONCE,
THE WATER WOULD BE ABOUT
4 FEET (1.2 m) HIGHER THAN A BASKETBALL HOOP.

LILY PADS CAN GROW TO BE WIDER THAN A KING-SIZE BED.

You can buy lollipops made with flecks of real 24-karat gold.

THE WORLD'S HEAVIEST INSECT, THE giant weta, IS BIG ENOUGH TO EAT A CARROT.

WHEN A KID LOSES A **TOOTH** IN GREECE, **HE THROWS IT ON THE ROOF!**

THE WORLD'S RICHEST MAN IS WORTH MORE THAN $60 billion— that's enough to buy a fleet of a million sports cars.

Every 50 years, rocks from Mars fall to Earth.

LEECHES CAN BE USED TO PREVENT BLOOD CLOTS.

Tomatoes were once thought to be poisonous.

Strawberry- and chocolate-covered Cheetos were sold in Japan.

WALKING USES 200 MUSCLES.

A CUDDLY ROBOT HAS BEEN USED IN EXPERIMENTS TO CHEER UP LONELY PEOPLE.

A **CAR** COULD DRIVE AROUND **EARTH** 8**7** TIMES ON THE AMOUNT OF FUEL IT TAKES TO FILL A JUMBO JET'S TANK.

Some
Greenland
sharks
may live to be
200
years old.

ONE OF THE WORLD'S LARGEST

ICEBERGS

IS BIGGER THAN NEW YORK CITY, U.S.A.

"TWITCHERS" ARE PEOPLE WHO TRAVEL AROUND THE GLOBE TO SEE RARE BIRDS.

Most frogs eat their skin after they shed it.

ONE SPIDER SPECIES SPINS A SILK BUBBLE AROUND ITSELF SO IT CAN BREATHE UNDERWATER.

THERE ARE NO COFFEE SHOPS
IN A TOWN CALLED
HOT COFFEE,
IN MISSISSIPPI, U.S.A.

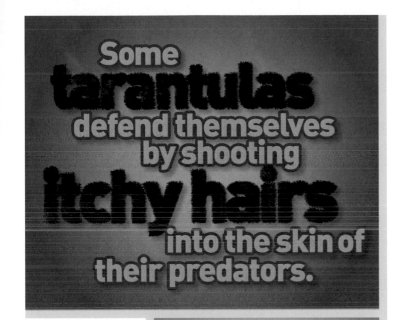

Some **tarantulas** defend themselves by shooting **itchy hairs** into the skin of their predators.

PEOPLE CAN BE **ALLERGIC** TO THE **COLD.**

The average **hug** lasts three seconds.

SOME TOADS CAN DETECT **EARTHQUAKES** BEFORE THEY HAPPEN.

When glass breaks, the cracks move

faster than 3,000 miles an hour. (4,800 kph)

A SEA OTTER HAS A MILLION HAIRS ON ONE SQUARE INCH (6.5 sq. cm) OF ITS BODY.

EXTRACTS FROM HUMAN HAIR ARE USED TO MAKE SOME PIZZA CRUSTS.

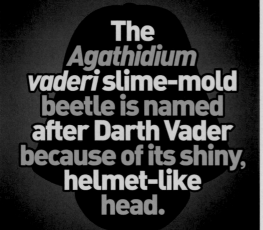

The *Agathidium vaderi* slime-mold beetle is named after Darth Vader because of its shiny, helmet-like head.

The **dwarf gecko,** one of the world's tiniest **lizards,** can fit on your **fingernail.**

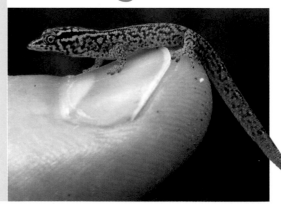

The **dot** over the letters **i** and **j** is called a **tittle.**

THERE ARE ABOUT
A TRILLION
WEB PAGES
ON THE INTERNET—
THAT'S ABOUT
140 FOR EVERY PERSON
ON EARTH!

PEANUT BUTTER WAS INVENTED AS A SOURCE OF PROTEIN FOR PEOPLE WITHOUT TEETH.

It takes **540 peanuts** to make one 12-ounce (340-g) **jar** of **peanut butter.**

ONE MAN DRIBBLED A BASKETBALL FOR 230 (370 km) MILES TO RAISE MONEY FOR JAPANESE TSUNAMI VICTIMS.

BARBIE'S FULL NAME IS BARBARA MILLICENT ROBERTS.

A LEOPARD WITH A STRAWBERRY-COLORED COAT WAS SPOTTED IN SOUTH AFRICA.

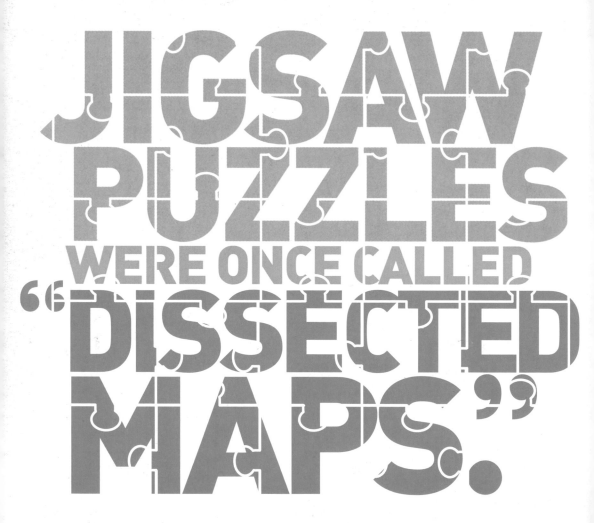

JIGSAW PUZZLES WERE ONCE CALLED "DISSECTED MAPS."

134

A WALRUS **TUSK** CAN GROW TO BE AS LONG AS A **BOOGIE BOARD.**

Some **cobras** can spit venom up to **6.5 feet**— (2 m) that's longer than one hockey stick!

AGOGGCHAUBUNAGUNGAMAUGG,
WORLD'S LONGEST NAME FOR A LAKE.

Your **heart** pumps enough **blood** in a day to fill **40 bathtubs.**

IF YOU COUNTED ALL OF THE HOURS ANGRY BIRDS **FANS** HAVE SPENT PLAYING THE GAME, IT WOULD ADD UP TO MORE THAN **200,000 YEARS.**

There is
no land on
Saturn.

You
can buy
socks
made from
bamboo.

A BLACK HOLE CAN WEIGH AS MUCH AS 10 BILLION SUNS.

IN MALAYSIA, PEOPLE TEXT "HA3" INSTEAD OF LOL.

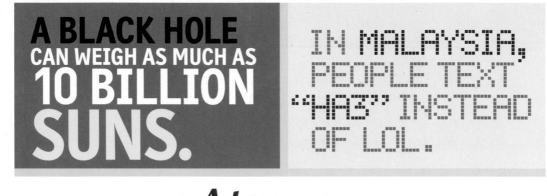

A toy car— dipped in *gold* and covered in *diamonds* and *rubies—* sold for **$60,000** at a charity auction.

SCIENTISTS GREW PLANTS FROM 32,000-YEAR-OLD SEEDS.

YOUR RIGHT LUNG IS A LITTLE BIGGER THAN YOUR LEFT LUNG.

A rainbow looks different to every person who sees it.

PEOPLE USED TO **CHEW** WILLOW **BARK** AS A PAIN RELIEVER.

Spider silk
has been used to make
violin strings.

56 MILLION YEARS AGO, **HORSES** WERE THE SIZE OF **HOUSE CATS.**

A **NEW** SKYSCRAPER GOES UP EVERY MONTH IN CHINA.

It's possible
to
snow
ski
on the
Big Island
of Hawaii.

A RESTAURANT IN THE UNITED STATES BUILT A GIANT CORNED BEEF SANDWICH MADE OF

150 POUNDS OF MUSTARD (68 kg)
530 POUNDS OF LETTUCE (240 kg)
260 POUNDS OF CHEESE (118 kg)
1,032 POUNDS OF CORNED BEEF. (468 kg)

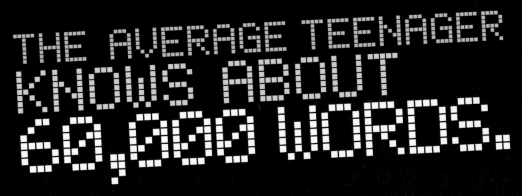

THE AVERAGE TEENAGER KNOWS ABOUT 60,000 WORDS.

THE TALLEST KNOWN
DINOSAUR,
SAUROPOSEIDON PROTELES,
WAS TALLER THAN A
SIX-STORY BUILDING.

A
giraffe
sleeps
1½ hours a day.

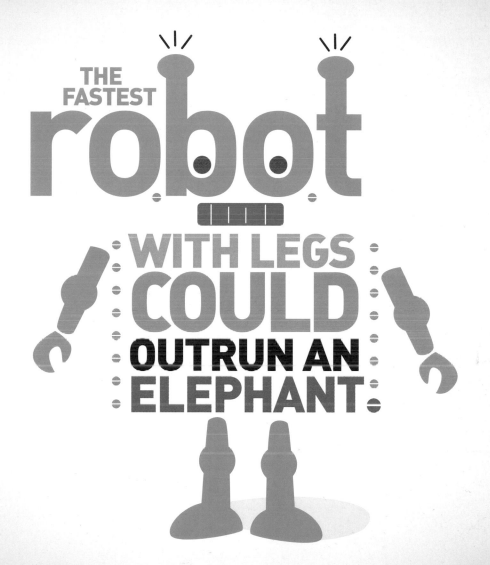

THE FASTEST **robot** WITH LEGS COULD OUTRUN AN ELEPHANT

THERE ARE OVER
A BILLION
MOTOR VEHICLES
ON THE PLANET.

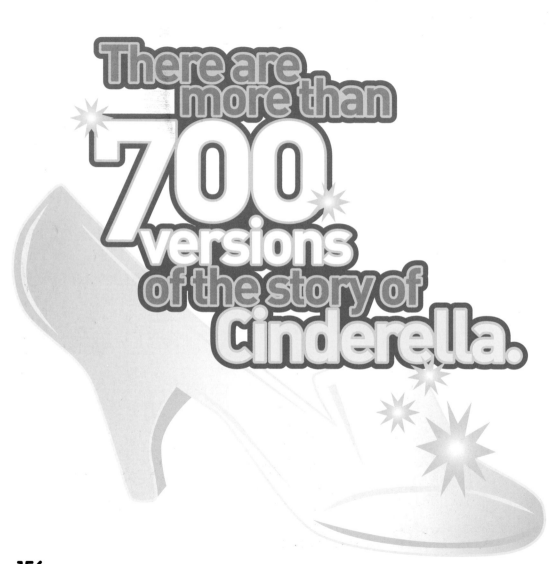

There are more than **700** versions of the story of **Cinderella.**

A GROUP OF MUSICIANS IN CHINA MAKES **INSTRUMENTS** OUT OF SWEET POTATOES, CARROTS, AND OTHER **VEGETABLES.**

A **BLUE WHALE'S** LARGEST VEINS **ARE SO BIG** YOU COULD SWIM THROUGH THEM.

There is a ski-up Starbucks at a ski resort IN THE UNITED STATES.

MAIL IS STILL DELIVERED BY MULE TO THE REMOTE TOWN OF SUPAI, ARIZONA, U.S.A.

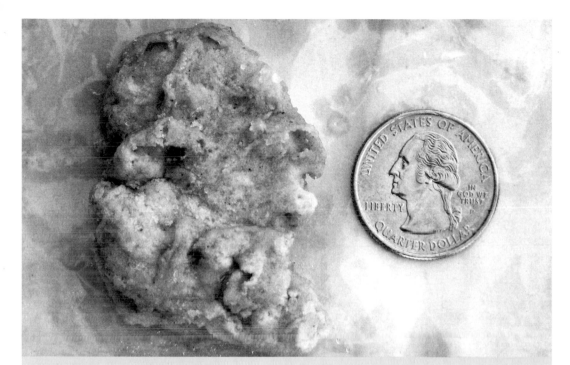

SOMEONE TRIED TO SELL A CHICKEN McNUGGET SHAPED LIKE GEORGE WASHINGTON'S HEAD ON eBAY FOR $8,100.

CHICKENS
WITH WHITE EARLOBES
LAY WHITE
EGGS;
CHICKENS
WITH RED EARLOBES
LAY BROWN
EGGS.

One **ostrich egg**
is equal to
two dozen
chicken eggs.

=

ABOUT
ONE IN A THOUSAND EGGS
HAS A **DOUBLE YOLK.**

A restaurant on a Spanish island is built on top of a **volcano**—and uses a volcanic hole as a grill!

The Atlas **moth** has a **wingspan** as wide as a **toaster.**

SOME FRUIT DRINKS GET THEIR **PINK COLOR** FROM THE **EXTRACT OF COCHINEAL BUGS.**

THE LEAVES OF A CERTAIN **PALM TREE** CAN GROW TO BE AS LONG AS **TWO STRETCH LIMOS.**

A CAT USES **TINY HOOKS** ON ITS **TONGUE** LIKE A **HAIRBRUSH** DURING GROOMING.

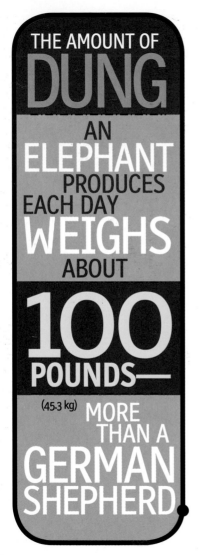

THE AMOUNT OF DUNG AN ELEPHANT PRODUCES EACH DAY WEIGHS ABOUT 100 POUNDS— (45.3 kg) MORE THAN A GERMAN SHEPHERD.

Rats are ticklish.

A helicopter engine is about the size of a backpack.

AN EXCITED **GUINEA PIG** JUMPS STRAIGHT **UP.**

You can buy **insurance** that covers alien **abductions.**

THE
SCARLET
IBIS
GETS ITS COLOR FROM THE
RED
CRABS
IT EATS.

One in **1,000** people can't smell a **skunk's** spray.

THAT'S WEIRD!

SOME PEOPLE WHO HAVE LOST A LIMB CAN STILL FEEL IT.

Moondust **smells** like burnt gunpowder.

IT TAKES 6 MINUTES TO MAKE A MARSHMALLOW PEEP.

More people live in the Tokyo, Japan, metro area than in all of Canada.

IT TAKES ABOUT 460 GALLONS OF WATER (1,741 L) **TO MAKE ONE HAMBURGER.**

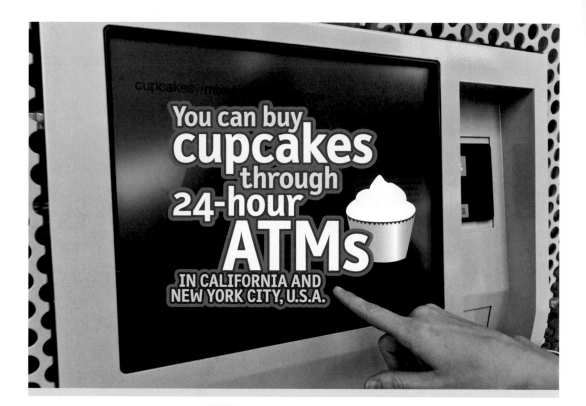

You can buy **cupcakes** through **24-hour ATMs** IN CALIFORNIA AND NEW YORK CITY, U.S.A.

CLOUDS FORM LOWER IN THE SKY TODAY THAN THEY DID TEN YEARS AGO.

TREES WITH SQUARE TRUNKS GROW IN PANAMA.

There's a foam replica of Stonehenge in Virginia, U.S.A.

One out of every **10,000 clovers** is a **four-leaf clover.**

BABIES BLINK ONLY ONCE OR TWICE EVERY MINUTE— ADULTS BLINK 10 to 15 TIMES.

A SWISS JEWELER CREATED A RING MADE ENTIRELY OF DIAMOND— INCLUDING THE BAND!

In China you can buy green tea ice cream flavored Oreo cookies.

PINK
IGUANAS
LIVE IN THE
GALÁPAGOS
ISLANDS.

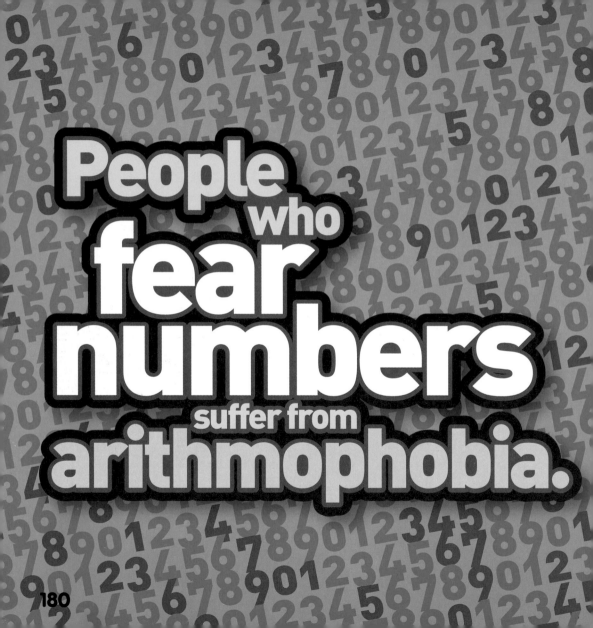

People who fear numbers suffer from arithmophobia.

ISTANBUL, TURKEY, IS LOCATED ON
TWO CONTINENTS:

EUROPE

ASIA

EUROPE AND ASIA.

A
squid
can change
its color and pattern
in 700 milliseconds—
almost in the
blink of an eye.

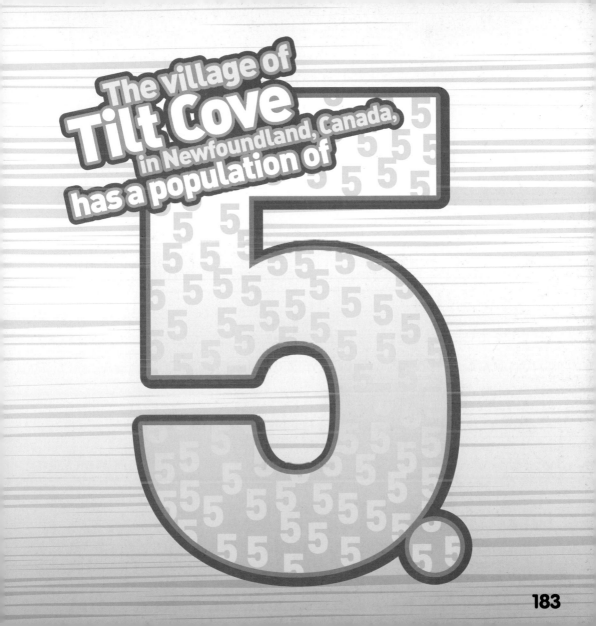

The village of Tilt Cove in Newfoundland, Canada, has a population of 5.

In the future, you may be able to take a space elevator thousands of miles (km) above Earth.

The technical term for the **pound sign** on a phone is **octothorpe.** **#**

THE TEN MOST POISONOUS SNAKES IN THE WORLD LIVE IN AUSTRALIA.

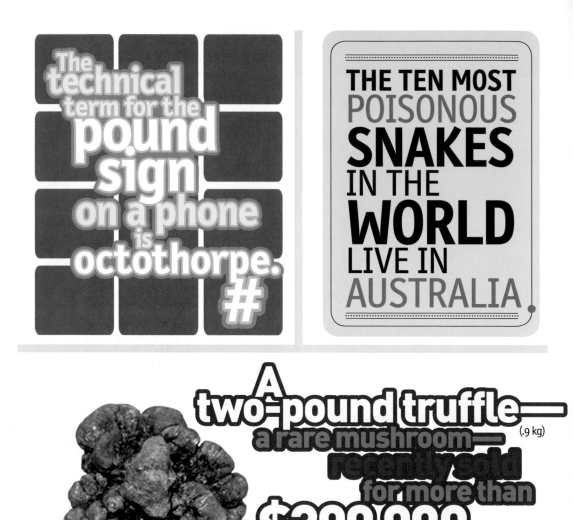

A **two-pound truffle—** (.9 kg) a rare mushroom— recently sold for more than **$300,000.**

The first bicycles didn't have pedals.

ONE IN
1,461
PEOPLE ARE
BORN ON
LEAP DAY.

The Olympic **flame** **travels with its own guards.**

AS YOU TRAVEL CLOSER TO THE SPEED OF LIGHT TIME SLOWS DOWN.

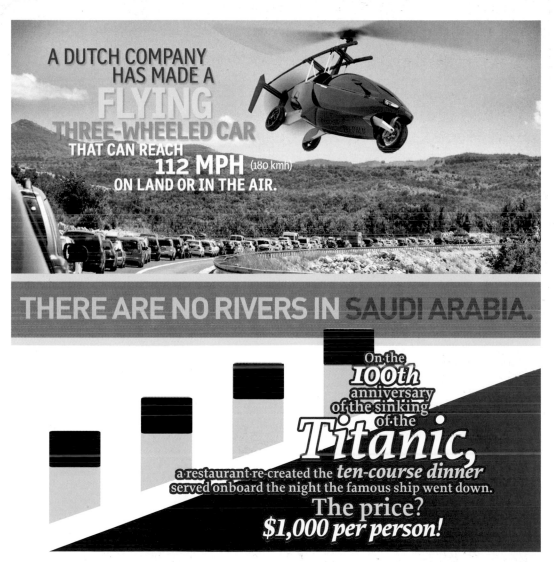

A DUTCH COMPANY HAS MADE A **FLYING THREE-WHEELED CAR** THAT CAN REACH **112 MPH** (180 kmh) ON LAND OR IN THE AIR.

THERE ARE NO RIVERS IN SAUDI ARABIA.

On the **100th** anniversary of the sinking of the **Titanic**, a restaurant re-created the **ten-course dinner** served onboard the night the famous ship went down. The price? **$1,000 per person!**

SCHNAUZER + POODLE

SCHNOODLE

THE WORLD'S LARGEST **GARDEN GNOME** IS TALLER THAN A GIRAFFE.

WORLD FAMOUS GNOME
NANOOSE BAY ESSO

THE **JACKFRUIT—** THE LARGEST FRUIT THAT GROWS ON A TREE— CAN WEIGH UP TO **110 POUNDS,** (50 kg) THAT'S THE WEIGHT OF 293 APPLES!

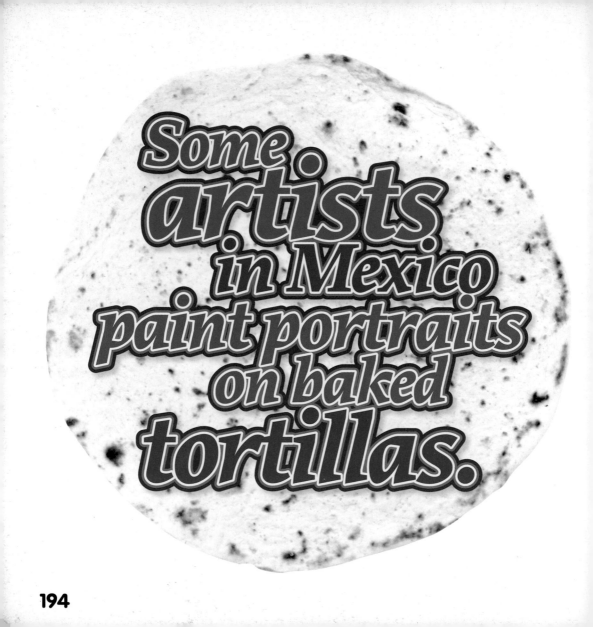

Some artists in Mexico paint portraits on baked tortillas.

TULIP BULBS WERE ONCE USED AS A KIND OF **CURRENCY** IN **HOLLAND.**

There's a **snail** that floats by making a **bubbly raft** out of its mucus.

YOU MAY SPEND UP TO HALF OF YOUR WAKING HOURS DAYDREAMING, ACCORDING TO ONE STUDY.

FACTFINDER

Illustrations are indicated by **boldface**.

The National Geographic Society is one of the world's largest nonprofit scientific and educational organizations. Founded in 1888 to "increase and diffuse geographic knowledge," the Society works to inspire people to care about the planet. National Geographic reflects the world through its magazines, television programs, films, music and radio, books, DVDs, maps, exhibitions, live events, school publishing programs, interactive media and merchandise. *National Geographic* magazine, the Society's official journal, published in English and 33 local-language editions, is read by more than 38 million people each month. The National Geographic Channel reaches 320 million households in 34 languages in 166 countries. National Geographic Digital Media receives more than 15 million visitors a month. National Geographic has funded more than 9,400 scientific research, conservation and exploration projects and supports an education program promoting geography literacy.

For more information, please call
1-800-NGS LINE (647-5463) or
write to the following address:
National Geographic Society
1145 17th Street N.W.
Washington, D.C. 20036-4688 U.S.A.

Published by the National Geographic Society
John M. Fahey, Jr., *Chairman of the Board and Chief Executive Officer*
Timothy T. Kelly, *President*
Declan Moore, *Executive Vice President; President, Publishing and Digital Media*
Melina Gerosa Bellows, *Executive Vice President; Chief Creative Officer, Books, Kids, and Family*

Prepared by the Book Division
Hector Sierra, *Senior Vice President and General Manager*
Nancy Laties Feresten, *Senior Vice President, Editor in Chief, Children's Books*
Jonathan Halling, *Design Director, Books and Children's Publishing*
Jay Sumner, *Director of Photography, Children's Publishing*
Jennifer Emmett, *Editorial Director, Children's Books*
Eva Absher-Schantz, *Managing Art Director, Children's Publishing*
Carl Mehler, *Director of Maps*
R. Gary Colbert, *Production Director*
Jennifer A. Thornton, *Director of Managing Editorial*

Staff for This Book
Robin Terry, *Project Manager*
Eva Absher-Schantz, *Art Director*
Rachael Hamm Plett, *Designer*
Sarah Wassner Flynn, *Editor*
Hillary Moloney, *Illustrations Editor*
Julie Beer, Michelle Harris, *Researchers*
Kate Olesin, *Assistant Editor*
Kathryn Robbins, *Design Production Assistant*
Grace Hill, *Associate Managing Editor*
Joan Gossett, *Production Editor*
Lewis R. Bassford, *Production Manager*
Susan Borke, *Legal and Business Affairs*

Manufacturing and Quality Management
Phillip L. Schlosser, *Senior Vice President*
Chris Brown, *Vice President, Book Manufacturing*
George Bounelis, *Vice President, Production Services*
Nicole Elliott, *Manager*
Rachel Faulise, *Manager*
Robert L. Barr, *Manager*